ISLAMIC RENAISSANCE

The Real Task Ahead

Dr. Israr Ahmad

English Translation

Dr. Absar Ahmad

Istinarah Press

2023 CE – 1444 H

It should be perfectly clear that the Qur'ān is only authentic in its original language, Arabic. Since perfect translation of the Qur'ān is impossible, we have used the translation of the meaning of the Qur'ān throughout the book, as the result is only a crude meaning of the Arabic text.

Qur'ānic verses appear in speech marks proceeded by a reference to the Surah and verse number. Sayings (*Hadith*) of Prophet Muhammad ρ appear in inverted commas along with reference to the Hadith Book and its Reporter.

Contents

Preface

The contents of this monograph were first published in the editorial columns of the June, 1967 issue of Monthly "Meesaq". Later on, in May 1968, it was published in booklet form by *Darul- Ishat-e-Islamia,* Lahore. Since then it has been brought out many times.

In this monograph, I have tried to present, to the best of my ability and comprehension, an in-depth analysis of the current religious and cultural attitude of Muslims all over the world. I have also discussed the nature of various movements working for the renaissance of Islam, their achievements and their shortcomings. On the positive side, my own prognosis for fruitful revivalist work has been expressed schematically.

On the basis of my analysis, I have also suggested a basic programme. As an immediate concrete step towards the realization of an Islamic revival, the plan for the establishment of a Qur'an Academy has been presented in detail.

After presenting this analysis and programme of action, I myself launched a vigorous struggle and movement for religious revival. With the grace of Almighty God, my humble efforts have borne fruit. For the concerted and collective pursuance of the goal of Islamic resurgence and especially for the establishment of the proposed Qur'an Academy, *Markazi Anjuman Khuddam-ul-Quran* was organized in Lahore. The proposals and plans delineated in this booklet have been fully incorporated in the constitution and objectives of the *Anjuman.* In fact some progress has already been made towards the establishment of the Qur'an Academy.

This monograph is being published for our readers by *Markazi Anjuman Khuddam-ul- Qur'an* who may take it as the *Anjuman's* manifesto. Even though many apparent changes have occurred in the Islamic world over the past few years, no substantial transformation in the complexion of the Islamic world has taken place. That is why it is being published almost as it appeared for the first time. Only a brief account of progress made so far in the establishment of the Qur'an Academy has been added in the last two pages.

Dr. Israr Ahmad
Founder President Markazi Anjuman Khuddam-ul-Qur'an
Lahore (Pakistan)

In the name of Allah, the Beneficent, the Merciful

Global Domination of Western Thought

The present age can rightly be described as the age of the predominance of Western philosophical thought and learning. The Western ideas about the nature of man and the universe are strongly upheld all around the world. Having taken shape roughly two hundred years ago, these ideas were continuously affirmed and reinforced by theorists and philosophers. Though politically, the present day world may be divided into a number of blocs, one single philosophical point of view prevails throughout. This attitude has colored all human civilization and culture at the global level. No doubt some alternative view points are also found here and there, but they are of marginal importance. The people, both in the Occident and in the Orient, who really have a say in public affairs, political as well as social and cultural, are without exception adhering to this viewpoint. The dominance of Western culture and philosophical thought is so pervasive and universal that even the point of view of such people as are struggling against it in some countries turns out on closer examination to be itself greatly influenced by the West. Indeed, they are themselves to a great extent Western in their approach and method and even in their purported ideology. They too think in terms of Western philosophy and ideology with the result that they lose their impact and efficacy to oppose it.

The Fundamental Point of View

The thought pattern which is operative as the basis of present-day culture and civilization was not hatched in a day, nor is it a simple and abstract phenomenon. Over the past hundred and fifty or two hundred years, European philosophers developed a number of schools of thought about the nature of man and human life, but one central attitude that persisted all through these variegated philosophical theories, and went on gaining momentum was the disregard for ideational and transcendental concepts. Concrete fact and physical phenomena became the core and object of human inquiry and philosophical quest. God, soul, and the Hereafter gradually disappeared from the spectrum of thought, yielding place respectively to discussions about the nature of the physical universe, matter, and human terrestrial existence[1]. Though at the academic level it was said that we neither affirm nor reject the doctrines about God, soul, and life-after-death, yet this avowedly agnostic position quite understandably led to the gradual elimination of these ideas from philosophical inquiry and discussion.

God has imbued man with many capacities and mental faculties to exploit to his benefit any field or domain, provided these faculties are properly applied. Every earnest research worker can explore a new world in the domain of his selected field of inquiry. Compared with the vastness and grandeur of the universe, the shining sun itself is nothing more than a tiny speck, while a tiny particle of dust may open up for a scientist realms hardly less in complexity and fascination than the shining sun. Similarly, the universe, matter, and terrestrial existence may look extremely trivial in contrast to God, the soul, and the life Hereafter, but if these mundane concerns are made the subject of study and research, they may lead to boundless vistas of knowledge.

This actually happened in Europe. When the universe and matter were brought under scientific investigation, man gradually discovered to his utter astonishment a clue to power and energy in apparently dead and inert material phenomena. And this led to a new revolution in the realm of knowledge and technology. A series of scientific discoveries led to greater control and exploitation of nature, and a wealth of new inventions made Europe an invisible power. The great impact and efficacy of the properties of matter became reason for focusing attention on physical laws in place of the spirit. As against the age-old discussions about God, His attributes, and spiritual entities, the physical universe and exploitation of natural forces were given prime importance in human inquiry.

Political and Ideological Onslaught of the West on the Islamic World

The newly acquired scientific knowledge and technical know-how gave to the West tremendous superiority in arms and military equipment. Its political power swept across the world in a very short time. Eastern nations and their governments crumbled before it like sandcastles. Since the Muslim states of the Near and the Middle East bore the brunt of this attack, the onslaught of the West struck Islam and Muslim nations the severest blow. The whole Muslim world was subjugated by Western imperialist powers in the matter of a few decades.

The West's occupation of the Islamic world was two-fold, military and political as well as ideological and cultural. However, since the European attack was primarily and initially political, the reaction against it in the Islamic world contained in its early stages a sense of revolt against political repression only. The painful realization by the Muslim world of the fact of European domination and the fragmentation of its own strength, either in the form of direct political rule and annexation or in the guise of indirect involvement and support of puppet governments, was expressed in heart-rending poems. The nostalgic memory of the glorious past and the passionate desire to regain the old strength and solidarity, indeed the desire to set the clock backward, expressed itself at one time in the volatile personality of Jamaluddin Afghani and at another in the form of *Tehreek-e-Khilafat* (*Khilafat* Movement)[2]. But reality prevailed over emotions and the political domination of the West became an established fact.

Immediately after consolidating its political hegemony, Europe started disseminating her ideological principles and point of view with a missionary zeal so as to capture and control the ideas and thoughts of Muslim nations. The material and scientific progress of the West had already dazzled the eyes of the world's conquered people. Moreover any superior nation must have some fundamental human qualities which help her to achieve her expansionist goals. The apparent evidences of Europeans' superiority contributed greatly to infuse defeatism in the minds of Muslims, and a vast majority of them began to appropriate Western ideas and values uncritically. Since the Europeans had themselves many schools of thought in the field of philosophy and social sciences, there was some scope of debate, counter-position, and selective adoption in these fields. However, since the findings of science had an element of certainty and its results were practical and tangible, they were not open to dispute. Science was therefore received with as much enthusiasm as should be accorded to Divine Revelation, and a large number of educated people in the Islamic world consciously or unconsciously accepted a secular and materialistic point of view. The entire Islamic world, including its deeply religious core, started giving more importance to material existence and worldly life, and less importance to God, the spirit, and the life Hereafter. A radical change of emphasis from transcendental themes to material and worldly pursuits occurred not only in Islamic society in general, but also in its religious leaders and scholars.

The Early Defensive Attempts and Their Achievements

The Islamic world made a number of attempts to meet the Western ideological onslaught, and many convinced and devout Muslims worked wholeheartedly to protect their faith and religion. These attempts to defend and safeguard Islamic values were of two types, the first was limited to mere protection and the second sought apologetic compromise and attenuation.

The merely defensive efforts to protect religious values and beliefs can be described, to quote Maulana Manazir Ahsan Gilani, as the following of *Ashab-e-Kahaf's* attitude. They fled from the mainstream of social life in order to hold fast to faith. Even though this might appear to be sheer escapist in motivation, it was in fact based on the realistic acceptance of the truth that the Muslim world was not able to mount a direct frontal offensive on the West. The only way that remained open was to keep away from the flood tide of secularism and hold fast to religious faith, caring little for those who derided this approach. As a matter of fact, whatever meager success was achieved in the defense of faith was made possible through this approach. The faith of a section of the Muslim community was saved from atheistic influences and a few candles of faith were left alight in the darkness of crass materialism. The structure of the faith and religious law was maintained through sermons and the teachings of the Qur'an and *Hadith*. The most important phenomena of this type of struggle in the Indo-Pak subcontinent was the establishment of a *Dar-ul-Uloom* at Deoband. In name a mere scholastic institution, it was in reality the harbinger of a great revivalist movement.

The fundamental principle of the more aggressive approach was to keep up with the changing times without loosing faith. To achieve this they undertook to sift the sound from the fallacious in modern ideas and to construct a modernist version of Islam in order to prove its veracity as well as its capacity to meet modern challenges effectively.

At first, signs of defeatism were manifest in those who took up this work. A number of pseudo-scholastic thinkers of India and Egypt started to test the fundamental tenets of the Islamic faith in the light of the new rationalism of the West. As a result of this, religious beliefs were attenuated and their metaphysical concepts were reinterpreted in purely scientific terms. Sayyid Ahmed Khan in the Indo-Pak subcontinent and Mufti Muhammad Abduh in Egypt and their acolytes attempted to formulate a modern interpretation of Islam to save it from anachronism and allow believers to make headway on the path of scientific progress like the Europeans. Their motives may have been sincere and their dedication genuine, but through these attempts Islam undeniably lost its very spirit and élan. The influence of Western materialism resulted in a non-religious version of Islam. Thus these attempts served only a negative purpose: saving of those who were already completely Europeanized in culture and life-style from being called 'un-Islamic'. Their inclusion in the fraternity of Muslim brotherhood remained unchallenged, and this new version of Islam was presented to the West on their behalf as an 'apology'.

The Development of the Social Sciences

The fundamentals of Western philosophy, disguised as suspension of judgment or agnosticism, were in fact the denial of God and the life Hereafter. They caused the physical universe to replace the transcendental concepts of God and soul from the center of human concern and inquiry. Numerous scientific discoveries and inventions naturally followed from this exclusive emphasis on worldly interests. Eschatological doctrines of life-after-death were completely rejected as topics of research in favor of the immediacy of worldly existence. As a result of persistent and exclusive thinking about the multifarious aspects of worldly life, a number of sociological and politico-economic theories were conceived and put forward. These theories gradually developed into full-fledged ideologies and world-views. Confined to strictly academic discussion in the earlier stages, these world-views were later made the social, political, and economic basis of nations. The age-old political systems based on traditional feudalism were replaced by nationalism, dictatorship, and democracy, and ancient economic systems by capitalism and socialism. A number of new political and economic movements emerged in the wake of these changes.

The Idea of an "Islamic Way of Life" and the Twentieth Century Islamic Movements

The world of Islam also received the impact of Western ideas in the field of social sciences, and Muslims began to propound Islam as a system of life. Islamic teachings were projected as an all- embracing 'system of life', and movements in different lands were launched to implement and put into practice this system of life.

These twentieth century revivalist movements started almost simultaneously in Muslim countries from Indonesia to Egypt. They were similar in a number of ways. Indeed it would not be far from true to say that they were all animated by a single conception of religion. It must be admitted, in all fairness, that these efforts imparted credibility to Islam as a code of life superior to other ideologies, and weakened the influence of the West upon the young.

There were other factors that helped to limit the influence of Western ideas and culture. The sweeping military and political victories of the Western colonial powers were checked with the passage of time and in many countries were met with forceful and sustained nationalist freedom movements. Consequently Western countries were forced to withdraw their political hegemony from occupied lands[3].

Though political influence and economic domination in the form of defense pacts or military and monetary aid programs are still very much there, almost the entire Muslim bloc has gotten rid of the yoke of direct rule by imperialist powers. In many Muslim countries nationalist freedom and self-rule movements were launched, and these invariably appealed to religious sentiments of the people for sparking off feelings of nationalism. There was no alternative to this, as Muslim nationalism had no anchorage other than Islam.

This appeal to religion, however, was more like a slogan than an existential concern for the Islamic faith. Yet it did strengthen the idea of the revival of Islam. At the same time, the hollowness of Western civilizations had been clearly brought out by the two disastrous world wars, causing even the West to consider the foundations of its own culture as ill-conceived and misguided. Materialistic atheism reached its logical culmination in the forms of socialism and communism, and moral as well as religious values were reinterpreted in purely economic terms. This alarmed Western peoples themselves, and they began to propound a new philosophy of humanism which was quite sympathetic to spiritual values. In the realm of science new physical theories[4] shook the very foundations of Newtonian physics and Euclidean geometry. Matter was no longer considered as something permanent and tangible, and the former absolute faith in mechanical laws gave way to less rigid views of the universe. This made it easier to affirm metaphysical beliefs, and gave support to religion.

Supported by these factors, movements for 'Islamic Renaissance', 'establishment of government according to the Will of God', and 'enforcement of the Islamic system of life' were started in various Muslim countries. Of all these, *Al-Ikhwan Al-Muslemoon*, which began in Egypt was the most prominent in point of quantitative strength and emotional fervor. The Indo-Pak subcontinent's *Jama'at-e-Islami* however, occupies a distinguished place among these movements, based as it is, on a solid and strongly defended thought-system.

These movements have been active in Muslim countries for more than thirty years and a substantial number of Muslim youth have been influenced by them. But it is an irony of history that practically none of these movements has achieved any remarkable success. Rather it seems as if they have outlived the span of their lives, and the moment is not yet ripe when the fond hopes for the renaissance of Islam can be realized. Egypt's *Al-Ikhwan Al-Muslemoon* has met almost complete disintegration within the country, and its few remaining members are scattered all over the Middle East and Europe. The Indo-Pak subcontinent's *Jama'at-e-Islami* fared no better, a greater portion of its potentialities having been spent up in the politics of Pakistan. At the moment it has hardly any programme other than joining hands with various political parties in the struggle for democracy.

One may think that the real cause of the failure of these revivalist movements lies in the impatience of their leaders. That is to say, they perhaps hastily, without first changing the minds of a considerable number of the country's intelligentsia, took part in active politics, which resulted in premature clash with the national leadership and the so-called 'progressive' elements. But in truth their failure is a direct result of their misconceived notion of faith and the error in their view of Islam.

The Error of their Interpretation of Islam

These movements' understanding and view of Islam are based on the same Western standpoint, preferring material existence and worldly pursuits to spirit and the life Hereafter. Though the metaphysical beliefs of Islam, which collectively constitute Islamic faith, are affirmed in their studies of Islam, they have not been properly stressed. Their gaze has been exclusively fixed on the teachings and precepts which Islam has laid down for the multifarious practical aspects of life and to which they have given the name of *Islami Nizam-e-Hayat* (Islamic System for Life). Their interpretation of Islam affirms all the religious beliefs but it lacks the inner state of deep faith in God (*Iman Billah*) which alone makes us know Him as the only absolutely powerful agent and the ultimate cause within us and in the cosmos. The belief in the Hereafter is asserted but it is practically devoid of the living faith, which was described by the Prophet Muhammad (SAW) when he commanded:

Live in this world like a stranger or wayfarer.

Similarly, the prophethood of Muhammad (SAW) is not denied, yet there is no real love or heart-felt attachment to him. For the more progressive elements, the Prophet had a role hardly higher than that of a postman or a leader of the social life of the Muslim community[5]. Even those who hold the *Sunnah* (practice of Prophet Muhammad (SAW)) as definitive and fundamentally important in religious matters, have created a loop-hole in it by making a distinction between *Sunnah adat* (habits) and *Sunnah risalat* (messenger-hood). This bifurcation has made it possible for its propounders to live freely at least their private lives in harmony with the fashionable trends of the times. In a word, faith is upheld only to the extent that suffices for one to be called a 'Muslim' in the legal sense of the term. The inner experience of faith that truly fulfills and validates the propositions of Islamic belief is not present. Indeed nobody seems to be aware of its importance and indispensability.

It is an outcome of this very standpoint that the practice of the Islamic faith has come to be regarded as synonymous with the State, and worship (*Ibadah*) simply equivalent to obedience (*Ita'ah*). The Prophet's statement that prayer (*Salat*) is the spiritual ascension of the believer is completely disregarded. The attachment of the human soul to prayer to the degree that it becomes the only source of inner happiness and peace is nowhere to be seen[6]. Contrary to this, the more progressive elements have identified the canonical prayer with the social order of the community. Some others assign importance to it only in so far as it is a comprehensive method for the organization of the Muslim community. The power of *Zakat*, the annul poor due, to develop and purify the soul is regarded as secondary to its role in the Islamic economic system or national welfare scheme. Fasting is commonly said to be an exercise in self control, but its potency to vitalize the soul by relaxing the shackle of the corporeal body upon it is either not fully realized or left unexpressed. The Prophet's saying, "Fasting is a shield"[7], is often reiterated in religious writings and sermons and a good deal of time is spent in its explanation. However, the holy tradition that "Fasting is for the pleasure of God and He will Himself grant its Reward"[8], is mentioned briefly and cursorily if at all. Similarly it is common knowledge about Pilgrimage that this provides the pivot of worship around which a vast universal brotherhood is organized. But its deeper religious significance and the spiritual blessings it brings are seldom expressed.

This new interpretation of Islam is a direct result of the universal domination of Western philosophical thought which has completely secularized the point of view of Muslims. Consequently the soul and its inner life is wholly discarded in favor of the affairs of worldly life which constitute the sole object of thought and reflection. This has resulted in a materialistic interpretation of faith and religion. Though at the theoretical level it is said that Islam is a comprehensive system of human welfare, concerned with both this world and the Hereafter. However, since their eyes are firmly fixed on the problems of this-worldly existence, Islam, in the final analysis, is reduced to a political and social system. Theological beliefs are considered as no more than a 'veil', a facade, or an outer crust[9]. The real mission they have set for themselves is the enforcement of this system of life and conduct. The yearning for communion with God, His adoration and humble supplication before Him, which are the real essence of worship, are relegated to a peripheral status[10].

The import of all these movements is more social and political than religious. They are more 'this-worldly' than 'other-worldly'. They are distinguished from other political and economic movements only in holding the Islamic way of life as a better solution to human problems than the systems of life enunciated by capitalistic democracy or communism. And this is tantamount to saying that the task of reviving the real values of Islam has yet not even started.

This is the reason why these Islamic revivalist movements are comparable to ships without anchors drifting to and fro on the waves. Quite often, they behave helplessly like a traveler who neither knows his destination, nor remembers his point of embarkation.

Revitalization of Faith: The Necessary Precondition of an Islamic Renaissance

Modern rationalistic and pseudo-scientific interpretations of Islam are quite alien to Islam itself and lack a direct link with the original mission of the Prophet (SAW). They are devoid of the spiritual message which is the heart of the Qur'anic revelation. They fail to appreciate Islam as a spiritual and metaphysical tradition. But since Islam is essentially based on inward faith known in Arabic as *Iman*, its renaissance can never be brought about without first reviving and indeed revitalizing the faith of a large part of the Muslim community. There is no denying the importance of political freedom and the independence of Muslim countries and these have undoubtedly contributed to generate greater awareness of Islamic values and ideals. Similarly, the idea of an Islamic way of life and confidence in its superiority over other ideologies has been useful to a limited extent and deserves our praise. The movements which were launched in the past, or those still engaged in advancing the cause of freedom are in fact contributing partially and in their own way, to the revival of the Islamic message. But the most real and fundamental task in this regard still remains to be done. It is imperative for the entire intelligentsia of the Muslim world to pay attention to - and whosoever realizes its real importance should strive for - the cardinal principle that a forceful movement be launched for reviving and revitalizing the *Iman* in the whole of the Muslim *Ummah*. In this way, *Iman* must be transformed from mere verbal attestation (*Qaal*) to an inward existential faith (*Haal*)[11].

Iman is essentially attestation of, and inner faith in, some metaphysical truths. The first step towards attaining this faith is to believe more firmly in some truths even though they are not observable or perceptible, and to hold the things heard by the heart to be more trustworthy than the things heard by the ear. Belief in the unseen (*Iman Bilghaib*) is the first and foremost condition of *Iman* and this requires a radical change in the thought system and in the point of view of the believer. According to this new perspective, the whole order of creation should be taken as nothing more than a fleeting appearance or shadow, whereas the existence of God should be felt as an eternally living Reality[12]. Contrary to the view that the universe is a chain of eternally present and uncreated causes and effects, or that the world is governed by 'natural' forces and rigid mechanical laws, the Will of God, His design and purpose should be 'seen' and felt in operation at all times and in all parts of the cosmos. Matter is looked upon as insignificant, and the soul is thought to be man's essence[13]. The locution *Insan* (man) is not to be attributed to man's animal and corporeal body but to the Divine spirit, the presence of which makes man superior to angels[14]. Worldly life should appear to be transitory and unreal, and life Hereafter should alone be taken as real and ever-lasting[15]. The pleasure of God should be held as more valuable than the attainment of all the riches of this world. And, according to a saying of the Prophet (SAW), the riches of this world should not even be assigned a value equal to a mosquito's wing[16]. Let it be clearly and distinctly understood that unless and until a major portion of the Muslim *Ummah* really undergoes this profound transformation in thought and belief, the vision and the fond hope of an Islamic renaissance can never be realized.

The most effective way to implant and inculcate faith in the hearts of the Muslim masses is the company and fellowship of such deeply religious persons whose hearts and minds are illumined by Divine knowledge and by the light of faith – persons whose hearts are untouched by conceit, hypocrisy, rancor, and avarice. It was through ceaseless evangelist and disseminating work, teaching and exhortation as well as practical examples portrayed through their conduct of life, that a continuous chain of pious and God-intoxicated people kept the beacon of faith burning after the collapse of *Khilafah ala minhaj al-Nubuwwah*[17]. Even though the winds of Western atheism and materialism are blowing high in Muslim lands, yet one can find here and there persons whose hearts and minds are full of certitude and staunch faith. The need of the time now is that the movement for Islamic faith and *Iman* be popularized and extended far and wide so that each and every inhabited piece of Muslim territory does have a few dedicated and selfless preachers whose sole aim in life is the pursuit of God's pleasure, individuals who, in obedience to the teaching of Prophet Muhammad (SAW), make religious and moral guidance of people their sole aim and ambition in life[18].

Fortunately, in the recent past there has emerged in the Indo-Pak subcontinent a mass religious movement, the impact of which is visible on a vast multitude of people. It has led them to a firm belief in Islam and the radical change of values that this entails. That is to say, the Creator, the spiritual existence, the human soul and the life Hereafter are held superior to the whole order of creation and worldly life. This movement is the *Jamaat-e-Tableegh.* It is an off- shoot of the movement of Deoband. It was founded and initiated by persons of deep and inner religious conviction. Although more than a third of a century has flown past, its fervor and emotional zeal has not abated a bit. Though we do not wholly agree with its approach and methodology, there is no denying the fact that it has brought about a complete change in the thinking of a great many people, who have started to feel that it is the Creator and not the created objects that should command our attention and that the uncaused first cause[19], and not the finite causes, is of prime importance. Similarly they develop a strong belief that it is not food or water but the Will of God that mitigates hunger and quenches thirst. Even the minor injunctions and precepts of the faith start appearing to them as of intrinsic worth and goodness without being grounded upon any logical argumentation or considered as part of a system of life or as a means to establish it. The smallest details of the Holy Prophet's (SAW) *Sunnah* appear to these people as pregnant with light (*Noor*) and splendor. They content themselves with the minimum material requirements of life and spend a major part of their time and energy in the propagation of Islam in their own way.

But as this movement addresses the sentiments and not the reason of the people and its main emphasis lies on action and not on understanding, its influence and efficacy is limited. The members of a community who hold reason and understanding to be superior to sentiments and action, remain uninfluenced by this type of preaching. The very mental constitution of these people compels them not to appropriate passionately anything that does not satisfy the test of reason and critical inquiry. They cannot attain the deeper levels of religious life without first untying the intellectual knots of their minds. These are the people who constitute the intellectual minority of a society and who command leadership over its ideology and policy. A change and indeed a total revolution in their viewpoint and way of thought is therefore of paramount importance. If *Iman* and belief could not be kindled in their hearts and they remained in the darkness of disbelief, faith occurring merely in the lower strata of society could not guarantee Islamization in a real and enduring sense.

The Real Task Ahead

For this reason the most essential task to be undertaken is to launch a high-powered academic movement which brings about a real change in the educated elite and intelligentsia of the society, taking them from the darkness of materialism and atheism to the light of faith and belief[20]. This movement should be aimed at inducing in them a worshipful attitude and a heightened self-awareness[21]. This objective can only be achieved at a strictly academic level through a cogently reasoned presentation of Islamic beliefs and a strong refutation of atheistic and materialistic philosophies. In this connection a point must be borne in mind. Since in our age fast means of communication have considerably increased mobility and the whole world can be looked upon as one human family, the aforesaid academic level of discussion will not be limited to one particular country. Rather it would be required to come up to the highest standard of sophistication found anywhere in the world. This colossal work must be extremely painstaking. But the vision of an Islamic renaissance which does not fulfill this requirement, is like living in a fool's paradise.

The first thing essential for this movement is to get in its fold such intelligent and talented young people who have a keen desire for knowledge and whose minds and souls are burning for the attainment of truth. These young individuals must experience an inner feeling that the ultimate reality is far from the realm of sensuous objects. The passionate desire in them for acquiring knowledge and discovering truth should be so intense that, paying no heed to petty cravings for worldly comforts and bright professional careers, they are prepared to dedicate all their lives for the achievement of this end.

These young dedicated research-workers will have to take a deep and critical look into the entire history of human thought from its earliest stages to the present day. Logic, metaphysics, psychology, ethics, and theology would become the central subjects of their study and reflection, though due attention will also be given to the social and physical sciences. Along with this thorough and critical study of human thought, it would be essential for them to study the Holy Qur'an, the last and most comprehensive Divine Revelation, in order to discover its truths. And if after a long and laborious study of human knowledge and Qur'anic wisdom, the beacon-bright message of the Qur'an becomes crystal clear to them, their minds and souls vibrate with its statements, the Qur'anic teachings about the nature of the outer world and of their own souls (*afaq wa anfus*) satisfy them completely and they experience an inner contentment as a result of this enlightenment, then they will have attained the true faith.

Only these individuals will possess excellence in true knowledge and wisdom. Instead of mental disruption and moral lewdness, their knowledge will lead them to greater fear of God's justice and punishment. Their personalities will be embodiments of the Qur'anic verse:

Only those fear Allah from amongst His slaves who are the people of knowledge. (*Al- Fatir*, 35:28)

Also their personalities and character will bear witness to the truth of a poetic line[22]:

No one knows this secret that a Believer,
Though looks like a reciter, is in reality Qur'an

The essence of the Holy Book lies in the particular gnosis which is called *Iman* or faith. No doubt the Qur'anic laws and precepts about the practical aspects of life are of immense importance in their own right. But compared with the essence which is constituted by its teachings regarding *Iman*, the legal aspects of the Qur'an are of secondary significance. Without the prior acquisition of this inner faith, deliberation upon the Qur'anic laws is of hardly any value. This point was very aptly conveyed in a statement of the Prophet's Companion, *Hadrat* Ibn Abbas (RAA):

We first learned *Iman* and then we learned the Qur'an.

The difficult task of refuting Western thought and rooting out its civilization and culture can only be executed in the real sense by those who have drunk deep at the fountains of wisdom and knowledge that flow from the Qur'an. It would be possible for these individuals to write a new 'Refutation'[23] of the philosophers of today and mount a crushing 'attack'[24] upon modern logicians. In a word, they will check effectively the flood of atheism and materialism which has been carrying away the human mind for the last two hundred years.

Besides this, they will have to undertake the positive task of initiating a new Islamic philosophical theology or *Kalam*, so that the facts discovered in the domains of mathematics, physics, astronomy, biology, and psychology may be assigned a proper place in the framework of Islamic beliefs. There is no inherent contradiction between the facts of these sciences and the tenets of *Iman*. The facts of physical sciences point partially to the same Absolute Reality which is comprehended through *Iman*. Forty years ago, Dr. Muhammad Iqbal set a precedence for this sort of work through the seven lectures published under the title, '*Reconstruction of Religious Thought in Islam*'[25].

The followers of Iqbal have, however, rather inappropriately concentrated on the nature of law, *Ijma'* and *Ijtihad* in Islam, which are in fact not directly related to the religious and philosophical aspect of his book. In fact his real purpose was the reconstruction and reformulation of the philosophical theology of Islam and his work is highly stimulating and thought-provoking in this regard. He did not claim that his word was final or perfect. He himself observed in the preface:

> As knowledge advances and fresh avenues of thought are opened, other views and probably sounder views than those set forth in these lectures, are possible. Our duty is to watch carefully the progress of human thought and to maintain an independent critical attitude towards it.

Therefore, if this task had been continued on lines suggested by Dr. Iqbal and some talented and dedicated individuals had devoted their lives to Qur'anic research, making it the hub and center of their intellectual activity, quite valuable and substantial work would have been produced by now. Until and unless a considerable amount of really good quality work is available in the field of Islamic theology or *Kalam*, the hope of instilling in the intelligentsia a deeply religious point of view can never be realized.

After the development and reformulation of religious and philosophical thought, the second most essential task would be to elaborate cogently in modern terminology the teachings of Islam regarding the practical aspects of life such as politics, jurisprudence, culture, and economics. In this connection, it was mentioned earlier that during the past forty years or so some commendable work was undertaken in Egypt and the Indo-Pak subcontinent. Both the *Jama'at-e-Islami* and *Al-Ikhwan Al-Muslimoon* have made 'Islamic way of life' and 'Social Justice in Islam' the central themes of their published work. However, this should only be considered as an appreciably good start in the right direction. It must be pointed out here that the current wave of plagiarism and publishing the old material under new titles will not at all serve the purpose. Pamphleteering by pseudo-scholars and immature writers and sale of publications among a particular group of people may bring economic benefit to a few but surely this will render no positive and lasting service to Islam itself. In the world of today in which people generally are pressed for time, persons of high intellectual caliber cannot possibly find time and leisure for superficial and second-rate literature. It is therefore imperative that whatever material is brought out, should be of high standard without necessarily being voluminous. For this task as well, besides critical knowledge of contemporary world affairs and social sciences, a deep and sound understanding of the Qur'an and *Sunnah* is called for.

A Blueprint for Action

Two things must be implemented immediately in order to launch the above-mentioned academic and Qur'anic research movement.

First, an organization should be established for the mass dissemination and exposition of the Qur'anic message. This organization should work for two objectives. It should strive to revive and revitalize the faith of Muslims in general, to enlighten their minds and chasten their character. It should also provide, through study circles and residential camps, practical training and guidance for the intellectual, moral, and religious enhancement of the people who respond to its call. It should convince those who sincerely aspire for an Islamic renaissance of the supreme importance of the academic movement referred to above. This organization should also earnestly look for such brilliant young scholars who are willing to devote all their lives in the academic task required for them. It is not an easy job to get hold of young and dedicated scholars in this age of exclusive pursuit of worldly gains. The problem of earning one's livelihood has become so acutely difficult today that most young people spend all their energies and potentialities in their professional career development. In our society, generally when a person is able to manage his basic necessities, he usually embarks on the never-ending process of raising his standard of life. But there are always in the world some pious and God-fearing persons. If some sincere and courageous people start this work with single-minded devotion, they are, with the help of God, sure to find many intelligent and capable youths, who will, in accordance with the Prophet's (SAW) tradition[26] make the learning and dissemination of Qur'anic wisdom the sole aim of their lives. The real need for the execution of a momentous task is always a strong inner urge for action which follows a particular emotion or idea. Once we have this inner urge, new possibilities or chances of success come up unexpectedly and the obstacles and the difficulties envisaged are overcome. What needs to be done is to propagate with missionary zeal the necessity of the

Islamic renaissance and revival. And if this is undertaken in the right earnest, there is no reason why this movement should not attract devoted and persevering workers for its noble ideals.

Secondly, a Qur'anic research academy should be established so that it may start a popular movement for learning and teaching the Qur'an among Muslims themselves, so that they may develop a fresh attitude of devotion to the study of the Qur'an. It is only when they come to cherish true faith and belief with a deep, inward conviction, that the light of the Qur'an will illumine their hearts and their feeling of reverence for the Holy Book will become profound. This academy should educate and train such young scholars who would have fully equipped themselves with both modern knowledge and Qur'anic wisdom, so that they may progress in the academic task before them.

The mass communication of Qur'anic teaching will result most importantly in drawing people's hearts to it. As their faith will strengthen, their minds will come more and more under the spell of the Qur'an and their feelings of reverence and devotion for it will become deeper.

Consequently, a large number of intelligent and capable youth will also be attracted to it, and quite possibly some of these seekers of knowledge will devote themselves to Qur'anic studies wholly and solely and make the learning and teaching of the Qur'an the sole aim of their lives. The major function of this academy would be to instruct and train those young people to become ardent workers for the cause of the Islamic renaissance. For this they will require a thorough knowledge of the Arabic language and its grammar and a refined literary taste to appreciate the beauty, force, and eloquence of its expressions. They should acquire a good grounding in the language in which the Qur'an was revealed by a critical study of the works of the renowned traditional writers. They should receive education in other religious studies, especially in tradition (*Hadith*), Islamic jurisprudence (*Fiqh*) and its principles. Every student who joins this academy should study as elective subjects one or more of the disciplines of social sciences according to his own taste and aptitude. It is only then that some of these scholars who are interested in philosophy and theology, would be competent to level, in the light of the Qur'an, reasoned criticism against contemporary philosophical positions and trends. In this way, they would initiate the new Islamic philosophical theology or *Kalam*. Thus these students of various subjects in modern social sciences would be able to carry out research on the Qur'an in the sphere of their own choice and present the light and guidance of the Qur'an effectively to others. Thus they would approach the intellect of modern man making a judicious use of modern terminology and sophisticated methods of logical reasoning.

End Notes

1 This shift from belief in metaphysical realities to the physical world is shown below:

Pre-Modern	Modern
Creator or God	Created Physical Universe
Human Soul	Matter or Body
Life Hereafter	Life in this World.

2 *Khilafat* Movement was organized by Maulana Mohammad Ali, Maulana Shaukat Ali, and Maulana Abul Kalam Azad in the Indo-Pak subcontinent for the revival of the Muslim Caliphate in Turkey, that was abolished in 1924. They started this movement in 1929 when they came out of jail. This mass movement created unprecedented agitation all over the sub-continent. The slogan of this movement was:

Spoke the mother of Mohammad Ali, Give your life oh son for Khilafah

3 The way the British Empire had to vacate her vast dominion one after another is an eye opener for any thoughtful person.

4 Reference is made here to Einstein's theory of Relativity and Bohr's Quantum theory.

5 Ghulam Ahmad Pervez is the leading exponent of this school of thought in Pakistan. The purpose to mention Mr. Pervez's thoughts here is to bring home to the reader the fact that this type of position is only the next logical step from the error inherent in most revivalist movements.

6 The Prophet's (SAW) saying:

means that I find inner comfort in *Salat,* i.e., the prayer offered five times a day.

7 The Prophet's (SAW) saying in Arabic is:

[8] Holy tradition (*Hadith Qudsi*) is that tradition in which God speaks in the first person through the Prophet. There are forty of these in all. The original Arabic 'holy tradition' quoted in text is:

[9] A statement to this effect has been attributed to a well known '*Kalamist*' (Theologian) and advocate of Islam. The actual statement reportedly reads: Islam is in fact a socio-political system onto which a 'veil' of theology has been placed.

[10] Even this state of affair is to be found in rather traditional and conservative Islamic movements. Otherwise the more liberal and progressive elements, under the impact of socialism and communism — the logical consequences of Western thought — have gone beyond calling Islam a socio-political system and regard it strictly as an economic programme. That is to say, for them Islam is co-extensive with a particular type of *nizam-e-rabubiat.* In the explanation of religious metaphysical beliefs and tenets of *Iman* they take their start from where Sayyid Ahmad Khan had gotten at through his rationalistic strain. By interpreting Paradise and Hell in terms of the well-being or otherwise of life here on this earth, and by interpreting *Qiyamah* (Judgment Day) in terms of atomic explosions, they have completely deprived Islam of its very spirit. In my view, this is only the logical terminus of the materialistic interpretation of Islam. A criticism of this view is not my objective here because even though it is given the label of Qur'anic thought it is undoubtedly gross, crass, and naked materialism and anti-Qur'anic in spirit. This incidental allusion to the so-called 'Qur'anic thought' has been made in order merely to show, as to what extent the secular version of religion can be pressed. A Persian verse depicts this situation very graphically:

If a mason lays the foundation in a wrong way,
The wall goes defective up to the summit.

11 The terms *Qaal* and *Haal* are often found in the literature of *Tasawwuf* or Islamic mysticism. Generally speaking, when the avowed attestation of *Iman*, something spoken and verbal, develops inwardly and permeates the entire being and activity of the believer, the *Qaal* deepens and enriches into *Haal.*

12 Dr. Israr has delivered detailed lectures on the reality of human worldly existence in comparison to the absolute existence of God in light of *Ayah* 3 of *Surah Al-Hadid*:

He is the First and the Last, and the Outward and the Inward: and He has full knowledge of everything. (*Al-Hadid*, 57:3)

These video lectures are available under the lecture series: '*A Selected Course of the Study of the Holy Qur*an, VE-9-35'.

13 Dr. Israr also quotes a sentence of Upanishad to put human material existence in its proper perspective:

Man in his ignorance identifies himself with the material sheets that encompass his real self.

14 This refers to the Verse 34 of *Surah Al-Baqarah* (2nd *Surah* of Qur'an), according to which God ordered the angels to prostrate before Adam.

15 In the Qur'an, the word '*belief*' is used for faith in God but the word '*certain*' is used for faith in Hereafter to stress its significance and importance in straightening human action:

"... for it is they who in their innermost are 'certain' of the life to come!" (*Al-Baqarah*, 2:4)

16 The prophet's (saw) saying is:

If in the sight of Allah the world had the value equal to that of the wing of a mosquito, He would not have allowed a disbeliever even to have a mouthful of water out of it.

[17] This is an alternative expression for *Khilafat-e-Rashida,* the 'Rightly Guided' Caliphate (*Khilafah*) of
Hadrat Abu Bakr, *Hadrat* Umar, *Hadrat* Uthman and *Hadrat* Ali (RAA).

[18] This refers to the saying of the Prophet (SAW):

If Allah guides a man to the right path through your effort and struggle, this is better for you than the costly brown camels.

[19] This is how philosophers have traditionally conceived of God as Necessary and Ultimate Being, existing independently and in its own right.

[20] Note the two quotations on the inside back cover of this book indicate that Maulana Abul Kalam Azad first had the idea of starting an academic movement in 1915. He proposed to establish *"Darul-Irshad"*

for this purpose. Later Maulana Abul Ala Mawdudi proposed to establish *"Darul-Islam"* for the same purpose.

[21] According to Qur'anic Philosophy, a true knowledge of one's own deeper self necessarily leads to awareness of the ultimate Self or God. There are also Prophet's sayings to this effect.

[22] A verse of Dr. Iqbal from the poem Mard-i-Musalman in Darb-e-Kaleem. *Kulliyat-e-Iqbal,* P.682. Fazlee Sons (PVT) Ltd, Karachi.

[23] This refers to Imam Ghazali's book '*Refutation of Philosophers*'in which he tried to refute the rationalistic philosophies of the eleventh century.

[24] Here the allusion is to Imam Ibn Taimiyya's book entitle '*Attack on the Logicians*' in which he criticized and conclusively refuted the arguments advanced by the logicians

of his time.

25 These lectures were delivered at the request of Madras Muslim Association by Dr. Muhammad Iqbal at Madras, Hyderabad, and Aligarh. They were written around 1928-29. The last lecture: 'Is religion Possible?' was delivered in a session of the Aristotelian Society, London, in December 1932.

26 The Prophet's saying reads:

The best amongst you are those who learn the Qur'an and teach and impart it to others.

THE AIM OF "DARUL-IRSHAD" PROPOSED BY MAULANA ABUL KALAM AZAD

"I was guided by the grace of Almighty Allah a few years ago to launch afresh a movement for disseminating the message of the Qur'an through "Al-Hilal". It happily resulted in a wide and popular reawakening of interest in Qur'anic teachings and methodology among both educated and uneducated Muslims. They felt renewed attachment and concern for the Holy Book. However, work on the second and more vital and arduous stage of this movement remains to be done, the work of educating a significant number of persons of the Muslim *Ummah* who follow the established guidelines of Qur'anic research and comprehend its wisdom fully. Only these highly enlightened and inspired Muslims can in turn start effective mass movement of Islamic revival and resurgence.

This is the sole aim before "*Darul-Irshad*". It will endeavor to accomplish the second stage of the movement of "calling people to the Qur'an" through encouraging and educating a group of Muslims as rapidly as possible. This group it is hoped, will perform the duty of popularizing the Qur'anic teachings on the widest scale and of starting a movement for the religious and moral purification of the *Ummah*!"

(Al – Balagh, November, 12/11/1915)

THE AIM OF "DARUL-ISLAM" PROPOSED BY MAULANA ABUL ALA MAWDUDI

"We have decided to assemble within the precincts of this institute persons well-versed in modern academic disciplines, and others who have a deep grasp of the religious sciences. These individuals must be of high calibre and intellectual capability. They will work under the guidance of a mentor, to be appointed shortly, who will be of excellent moral character. Besides having attained deep and full insight into the wisdom of the Holy Qur'an, he will know in detail about modern revolutions and changes in various realms. He will work to acquaint these people with the spirit and elan of the Divine Book and the Prophet's (SAW) *Sunnah*. He will also help them in reconstructing the manifold aspects of Islamic thought, including Philosophy, "*Hikmah*", Morality, Political Science and Economics, so that through their scholarship and missionary work they can struggle to revive the pristine glory of Islamic civilization."

("Iqbal, *Darul-Islam* and Mawdudi, p82)

www.ingramcontent.com/pod-product-compliance
Lightning Source LLC
Chambersburg PA
CBHW062204160726
48282CB00027B/990
* 9 7 8 9 3 9 4 8 3 4 1 9 4 *